The Legacy *of an*
IMMIGRANT WOMAN

Unmasking the opportunities available but hidden in plain sight that will lead to success in a new and strange land

FRANCISCA RAMONI, PH.D.

ISBN-13: 9781686290343

Dedication

To my daughters: Bellie, Renee and Dana

You are beautiful, intelligent and caring.

Read hard, work hard, the world is full of possibilities.

Respect others and self, and most of all, spend time with GOD.

Never forget your roots.

"Education is for improving the lives of others and for leaving your community and the world better than you found it."
- Marian Wright Edelman

Preface

Who is an Immigrant?

The word "immigrants", as understood in the United States (U.S.) immigration law, are persons admitted as legal permanent residents of the United States. In laymen's terms, an immigrant is a person who leaves one country to settle permanently in another.

Once admitted, immigrants are subject to a few restrictions. For example, they may accept and change employment, and may apply for U.S. citizenship through the naturalization process, generally after five years.

There are approximately 21 million female immigrants who live in the United States, which is just 13 percent over the nation's female population. Immigrant women come from all over the globe, and they come to the U.S. in multiple roles: students, professionals, spouses, parents and caregivers.

In as much as they come in multiple roles, the immigrant woman makes an important contribution to local communities, the economy, and society.

This book is written with the immigrant woman in mind. There are so many opportunities available to you, you just have to know where to go to find them, and take full advantage. Success is just a button away, once you have done the proper research.

Table of Contents

The Legacy *of an*
IMMIGRANT WOMAN

Unmasking the opportunities available but hidden in plain sight that will lead to success in a new and strange land

FRANCISCA RAMONI, PH.D.

1

Landing in the United States of America

"One of the most courageous things you can do is identify yourself, know who you are, what you believe in and where you want to go." – Sheila Murray Bethel

I have always dreamed of coming to America to pursue my doctorate education. I heard a lot of stories about all of these opportunities in America—how you can further your education, and at the same time, get a job to support you while you are going to school.

I thought my doctorate dream would come true if I came to the United States of America. One thing I knew for sure was that I was not going to the United States without proper documentation, or as we call it 'papers'. I decided to look for schools, do my research and apply for student loans and scholarships. I wanted to be as prepared as possible before I even left my country.

My doctoral dream started while in India as a student, but it didn't last for long. I enrolled for a Doctorate program, paid my first semester fees, attended one week of school, and was about to buy my school supplies. Then the phone call comes from my dad, "I know I gave you a go ahead to register for your Ph.D. program, but looking at the situation, I would like you to come back home and help me educate your siblings."

My heart sunk, I was confused, and I did not know what to do. Without thinking I said, "Yes, daddy, I will be coming home as soon as I get my plane ticket." Soon after that call, I got my ticket, packed my stuff, bid bye to my friends and professors, and left for Kenya. All the while I was telling myself that no matter what, I must complete my doctorate.

Back in Kenya, I got myself a job; and after two years of being on that job, a friend persuaded me to apply for a green card lottery. I discussed it with my husband, and he was a bit skeptical about the whole thing. I reminded him about my dream of completing my Ph.D. and that this could be the best opportunity for us if we would happen to win the green card lottery.

My husband got on board and so the following day, with the help of my friend who was already in it, I went ahead and submitted my application for the green card lottery. It took about two years. By the time we won the lottery, we had two kids.

My husband and I discussed the probability of giving our girls a better opportunity in terms of schooling and quality of life. We based our discussion on what we had heard about the U.S., which now I know was NOT the reality. The only thing we were sure of was that we had proper documentation and therefore we would be able to get work and support our young family.

We wanted a better life for ourselves and so we took the risk. I now call it a 'gamble'. We processed our papers in preparation for the visa interview, which we passed and was ready for the United States of America.

Moving or relocating to America is both financially and emotionally draining. The process costs a lot of money and sometimes you may need to sell some of your properties or get a loan in order to complete it. I am talking about something as small as mailing the completed documents back to the United States to Visa fees to medical examination fees, and finally the airplane ticket—which is the most expensive.

If you do not have a good income or a good support system, it is very hard to make it to America, even when you have won the lottery. Just to let you know, submitting an application for a green card is free. The medical tests are way too expensive but you cannot move forward without them.

Emotionally, you must be very strong to leave all your family members, relatives and friends to go to a foreign land. You leave all that you have known, and all the legacy you have built for yourself. It is very hard when you think about all you are leaving behind when going to an unknown place.

When I was about to leave, I cried almost every day, just thinking about leaving my parents and siblings. I thought that I might not see them again. I was worried about who would provide support for them in my absence. So many things could happen while I'm not there. I worried so much about my parents and how I would be able to care for them while I was far away. It was really an emotional deal for me.

I just thought about all the support systems I would be leaving behind, including my house help. How was I going to manage work and children on my own, more specifically in a foreign land?   I am used to having almost everything done before I get home from work, but now I would be doing all this by myself when I got home from work in America. Who is going to watch my girls while I am at work? Do I leave them behind, or do I bring the house girl—and if I did, what was going to be the procedure?

How about the household goods… what was I going to do with them? I had bought a very expensive carpet and curtains just a few months back, which I had gotten attached to, now I was going to leave all this behind.

I also got emotional when I thought of transporting all my stuff back to the rural area. Who was going to care for it? Are they going to be safe? My wedding stuff, clothes, shoes, and gifts which I had not opened. I was emotionally drained to the extent that a week before my departure I could not eat or sleep. A couple of times I got sick and developed anxiety. I was emotionally drained at the thought of me leaving my home, what I had built for the last four years, my job, friends and family, plus the fear of unknown.

In October 2005, I landed in Texas, United States of America (USA) with my two daughters—the youngest was barely one-year-old and strapped on my back, and my 4 ½ years old holding my hand and walking across the airport through immigration.

When we stepped out of the airport, it was cold and windy and my mind was racing. How I was going to survive here with my family in such weather? We were lucky that we had a family when we got to the USA, and that made our settling much easier. Also, my husband had been here one month prior.

After a week or so, the jet lag was finally over and we settled in. We got used to the going in and out of town, enrolled my oldest daughter in school, while I stayed home with my youngest daughter, and the host family and my husband went to work.

Staying at home was not easy, mainly because I had an 8 to 5 job back in Kenya, as well as doing a side hustle. My side hustle back in Kenya was selling rice as well as second-hand and new clothes; so staying in the house a whole day was not my thing.

Back home I had a household staff who would stay with the girls, do all the house chores, cook, clean and help the girls with their homework. It was normal for us to have a driver, a maid (or sometimes two) and a lawn maintenance person who we call a gardener. Back in Kenya, we have a good family support system. Everywhere you turn, you can always get help. Your neighbor can help you with the kids, food and even a ride to work.

The system in the United States is very different. Here you do everything by yourself. No support system like back home. So I decided to get myself in a routine. Once everyone left the house, I would prepare my daughter, pack her food and a diaper bag, and walk to the library which was not far from where we lived.

I met some wonderful mothers who brought their young ones to the library activities and we became friends. Our kids would play together while we were on the computer doing different things. For me, I was busy looking for a job; some of the ladies gave me names of websites that I should visit to look for jobs.

Being at the library was one of my best moments of the day. I would apply for jobs, did some online courses and when I was tired, turned to social media for a break or watched local and Kenyan news. I found myself so busy at the library that, before I knew it, it was 2:30p.m., time to go pick my other daughter up from school.

I was so excited when I finally found a job in a call center where I did collections for credit card customers. That was very interesting to say the least. Little did I know that job was going to turn into a nightmare.

The customers were abusive and spat out racial remarks. Being new to this country, I really felt violated. One time a customer told me, "Go back to your country. Are you calling here asking for food?" That was the turning point. I told myself I deserved better and, after two months in collections, I was promoted to another department where I was no longer on the phone.

That promotion did not quench my thirst for bettering myself and doing better. I promised myself to remember that this is not what I wanted to do for the rest of my life.

2

Settling In A Strange Land

"Education is the most powerful weapon which you can use to change the world." – Nelson Mandela

My dream has always been to complete my education by earning a Ph.D. My pursuit for my dream started when I came to America. I researched colleges of my interest and the pros and cons of different schools, and why I should attend one college and not the other.

Other things of importance to me were: the cost of the school; how the school ranked in the nation; how it ranked in the discipline I wanted to study; the proximity to school from my job and my home; flexibility of the program; the type of classes they offered; are they only face-to-face classes or do they offer online classes too; do they offer weekend and evening classes; do they offer daycare facilities on sight, if not can they work with me with my schedule and my children; how friendly are they to non-traditional students?

The research took a while and when I was ready, I discussed it with my family. We reached an agreement and enrolled in one of the local universities.

In 2010, my school life began and it was not easy. When I think about the things I did not know and should have known before enrolling in school, it was mind boggling! There was so much I did not know, even with all of my research I had done prior to choosing the school.

I wanted to go to school as early as I arrived in the United States, but did not know how I was going to pay for my tuition. So, I decided to save money and have at least two semesters' tuition amount on hand. Now thinking about it, I wonder how long it would have taken me to save and fund my entire education?

In my venture to research how I can fund my education, and asking around, I come to learn that I can enroll in school and apply for FAFSA (I'll talk more about this in the next chapter).

Loaded with all the financial information I needed, I enrolled in a school and applied for FAFSA. Once my application was submitted, I went ahead and applied for grants and scholarships, too. This empowered me to go back to school now that I figured out how to cover the costs.

I started school and, after one year, I realized that I could also apply for departmental and university grants as well as scholarships. Thereafter, throughout my schooling, I made sure I applied for all monies available for students. Please do not leave any money on the table! I was so fortunate that I got all the grants and scholarships I applied for, be it merit or financial need-based funding.

I also made sure I engaged my family, friends and church members on my journey. I knew I would need their support along the way. And true to my thinking, family, friends and church members became my support system.

The family, especially my daughters, made it easy because they followed the routine without fail. They helped in the house with house work, and did their homework without me having to follow or push them around. Sometimes I would bring them to school for my classes and they would sit at the back of the class and do their homework.

There were even days they would stay with me in the library for long hours. They would be reading or finishing their homework, we would take breaks, go for walks and sometimes play games outside the library if the weather was good.

When I left the house on Saturday, I left equipped with a change of clothes, blankets, board games, a basketball, food and sometimes even medication, you just never know.

The support I got from friends and relatives was overwhelming, more specifically during my exam season. If the exam was on a weekend, I would drop the girls off at church or somewhere for an activity, and they would pick them up and either drop them home or I picked them from their home.

The church support consisted of church activities and camps which I was not able to attend due to exams. I never wanted my girls to miss anything because of my schooling.

One thing which also made my schooling smooth was the school I was attending. The school was very supportive; they allowed me to attend with my girls sometimes. Since I was working full-time, I could come in late after picking up the girls. The school was a big part of my success. And I believe that it was because of my research I did prior to enrolling that made the difference. Knowing which questions to ask helps when making long-term decisions. And it paid off!

3

Building A Solid Support System

"What you get by achieving your goals is not as important as what you become by achieving your goals." – Zig Ziglar

As an immigrant, your support system is very important —not only when you are pursuing your studies, but just in general. When you are away from your country of origin, a good support system will make a big difference in your life. It will make your life easy or hard, depending on the circle you are in or the people you surround yourself with. With that being said, choose your support system, friends, circle wisely.

Make sure they align with your goals, dreams and aspirations. When you have children, this support system will help with instilling the values and beliefs of one's culture as children interact with one another learning from each other. During this interaction, the children may be able to better understand their identity and cultural beliefs, more specifically if there is a grandparent around.

If you are going to school, please find a school that will be supportive, talk to them about your situation (i.e. you have children, you are single or if you need financial help). Ask fellow students if the professors are understanding and would work with you. I understand some schools have daycare centers for students, find out. What I am trying to say is do a thorough research before enrolling in a school.

I was lucky and blessed that I got a lot of support from not only friends, family and church, but the school too. There were days I would go to school with all three girls. The younger one was playing with her toys at the back, while the other two were doing their homework in the lounge where I could see them.

Helpful Tips for Survival

What I learned throughout my journey through school was that you need to speak up if you need help. Help will come when you ask for it, just **be patient**.

You got to be patient with everyone around you. Yes, you may have things due and papers to write, but have patience and understanding—especially with your family because there are times things will be going west and you could get frustrated.

Take it easy on them. As a student, mother, wife, and a full-time employee, I had to master some skills that would help me navigate this season of life I had chosen. **<u>Time management</u>** is one of those skills. I had to master this skill in order to get organized and move the puzzles in the right direction at the right time.

I had to manage my time wisely to be successful in everything I was doing during that season. I also made sure my daughters had some of these same skills because we were working as a team and we could not afford to waste any time. Therefore, everything we did was on a time clock.

<u>Positive attitude</u>—I had to be positive all the time. I can tell you it was not easy, but If I wanted to succeed, I had to have a positive attitude all the time.

There were days I would get frustrated either with myself or the girls, and I realized early in the journey that would not work. Therefore I decided to have a positive attitude in everything.

I am proud to say that decision made my life stress free. I would listen to my girls when they were frustrated and uplift them with a positive vibe. And if I was frustrated, they would also give me some positive words.

At the end of year two of my schooling, we laughed off any frustration and just soldered on. Our mantra was "this is a passing cloud, we are going to make it."

I also taught my girls to be self-motivated. If it needs to be done, anybody and everybody can do it. So, everyone did everything. If you are done with what you are doing and there is something pending, you just do it —especially if it was housecleaning and cooking. This is what a family unit is all about.

My daughters became my best friends and partners in this journey. We knew the routine and it ran so very well and smoothly that the only thing that would divert us from our routine was if one of us got sick. God forbid if it was me!

The home calendar was updated and we reviewed it every Friday. The calendar had parents/teachers' conferences, track meets, basketball tournaments, friends' birthdays the girls wanted to attend, TV time and movie night. We developed a plan together as a family, and we were all accountable to making it work.

Finally, I graduated with my Ph.D. and had the urge to empower my fellow immigrants who were thinking of going back to school. This is my story; this was my journey, and my hope is that my book will be an encouragement and a roadmap to success for any immigrant who is aspiring to go to school.

My main goal here is to show the immigrant individual, be it a father, mother, married or single, that going to school is doable, manageable and will eventually payoff.

Therefore, I shared my journey and below, I will try to share as much as I can about the tools and information that helped me so that it may help you navigate this journey.

By all means, this is not an all-inconclusive set of tools and information. I encourage you to do more research before you enroll in school. This list is what I did and what worked for me.

Here are some suggested tidbits that you need to know and do to succeed in your schooling journey. I hope this information is going to be useful, not only to adults who want to go back to school, but this can also be useful to immigrant parents whose children are planning to or about to go to college.

It's imperative as an immigrant parent to know that you have all of these resources to help you and your children get the education you need or deserve, utilizing the financial support available out there.

4

A Higher Learning: Funding Your Education

"My strength is knowing who I am and where I came from, my island." - Oscar dela Renta

As an immigrant, whether you are a graduate or not, when you land in the USA, it is imperative that you get American academic credentials. This can be either going to college to get a degree or certification. Your foreign credentials do not really count.

Most American organizations may not recognize your foreign credentials and correlating it with American credentials is difficult. In most cases, most immigrants end up getting entry-level jobs, even though they were mid-level to senior managers back in their countries. This is really frustrating especially if one was doing well and had a great position back in their country of origin.

This frustration brings about a lot of mental health issues in some, and others just decide to give up and return to their country. Some immigrants have changed their careers just to fit in and make ends meet. It is interesting to say they really like their new careers. It is very hard for one to move with the whole family to a foreign land thinking that things will be better, only to come and face such roadblocks.

The other challenge immigrants face is the ability to finance their education while here, especially when you are still new and trying to settle down. Can you imagine you are new in a country, or even a new town, trying to get things in order and the thought of paying tuition or even going back to school? This gets tougher and tougher as time goes by. There are various avenues for immigrants to navigate this journey called life in America and come out successful.

"Education is the passport to the future, for tomorrow belongs to those who prepare for it today."-Nelson Mandela

One avenue which I really want to address is the going back to school and how you can get your tuition paid off. There are organizations that will pay for your tuition from day one of your employment, and others that may do so after a certain number of months or years on the job. Either way, there are employers who provide educational benefits to their employees.

As immigrants, funding our education has been the biggest challenge when establishing a new life in America. But I encourage you to look at the glass half full, instead of half empty. If you want it that bad, you will find ways to finance your education. Here are five suggested ways/sources one can pursue when funding their education. Most students use a combination of two or more of the sources that I will talk about below.

Federal Aid

This is a type of aid that may be appropriated through grants, loans, or work study. Any college student can apply: undergraduate, graduate or professional. The benefits of this type of aid is that you get a lower interest rate and flexible repayment terms.

Federal Aid is a United States government type of funding that is available solely to students attending post-secondary education. This funding is used to cover many costs which students may incur in the process of their education. In order to qualify and get financial aid, you have to complete a free application for Federal

Students Aid (FAFSA)—remember I mentioned this earlier? Completing a FASFA application is a part of the financial aid process, you cannot get any education financial funding from the government unless you complete the FAFSA form.

The FASFA application open doors to many other financial sources of assistance, such as grants and scholarships. Grants (such as the Pell Grant) and scholarships are money you don't have to pay back. However, if you take loan money, you will need to pay it back once you graduate. You can also apply for work-study jobs, too. You can work at the school you're attending, and part of the money earned can be used to pay part of your tuition.

Once you have completed the FASFA application and the money has been disbursed to you, you need to start attending classes. Once you have financial aid funds, do not drop classes or stop going to college; however, if you must, then make sure you contact the financial aid office at your school. It does not matter whether you drop classes, stop going to college or fail your exams. Keep in mind that any funds received from financial aid, must be paid back.

Deciding to attend college is not an easy one, and neither is stopping. Bear in mind that you cannot just go in and out of college as you wish because financial aid has a cap to the hours you can take for any course; and currently, they have also capped the amount you can receive.

In addition, if you have grants and you drop out of school you will be asked to start a repayment plan to repay a portion of the grant award. When you are awarded financial aid, you may end up having leftover money—this can be used for personal expenses (food, transportation, bills and books) or you can request the school to keep the money for the school year. Just in case you need it later, the school can give it to you.

Also you can advise them to return it back to the lender at the end of the school year. If you ask the financial aid office to send the funds back, you will not incur any interest on the leftover loans.

State Aid

These types of aid are grants, scholarships, work-study funds, state loans and tuition assistance. This applies to undergraduate and graduate students and the benefits are they reduce the cost of attending a state school. You can find more information through your school or financial aid counselor of the school you plan to attend. In addition, you can contact the state's financial agency.

Institutional Aid

Institutional Aid comes directly from the college you are in or planning to attend. In some instances, the aid is actually from individuals or alumni, and they donate the money directly to the school.

These are usually given through grants that are available to undergraduate and graduate students. They are awarded and provided based on academic merit or financial needs, and do not need to be paid back. This type of grant is easily found on the school website.

There are also departmental grants which you can locate on the department website. Therefore, it is important for you to check at the beginning of the school year—most of them have a deadline for March.

Immigrants can easily apply for and get this grant. We just need to get the good grades and be in a good standing status at the school. You can also talk to your advisor or the department chair about your financial needs so that they can help identify any grants that may be available for you.

This is one of the many things I learned while I was going to college. Sometimes we immigrants are very shy about telling people what we are going through, but I learned that if you don't ask, no one will readily offer this information to you.

If you don't talk to someone, nobody knows what is going on with you and you may never get the help you need. It took me two years to learn about the department grants and when I knew about them, I never stopped applying.

For the next 5 years, I received the departmental grants until the day I graduated. The beauty about this is that you don't pay them back. One thing you have to keep in mind is that institutional aid is very competitive due to the limitation of funds, therefore it is very important to check all the requirements and make sure you meet them before submitting your application.

Private Aid

These are private student loans or scholarships and are available to undergraduate, graduate and professional students. The private loans have a variable APR (annual percentage rate), you must have a cosigner, and it also helps build credit.

Scholarships

Scholarships do not need to be paid back. There are certain websites you can go to find private scholarships.

Unigo is one of the websites where such scholarships are offered. Visit www.unigo.com for more information.

For the scholarships offered online, a student has to be careful and do a lot of research to find which one you may qualify for, and also be careful of scammers.

Education Assistance

Many companies currently offer education assistance as one of the benefits to the employees so that they can retain top performing talent. This benefit includes education reimbursement for employees to earn their degree.

Most companies have an annual cap per school year. The companies usually require that you register for a class that is related to the companies' line of business. You must also pass your classes in order to get reimbursement.

Some companies have a certain GPA requirement to get reimbursement. You have to also perform well at work and have a good performance review rating. Do your research and be sure the college you are planning to attend is an approved college that the company would sponsor.

Your manager has to approve or sign off that you can go to college and also the manager is the one who will sign your reimbursement request to the human resources department. The most important thing is making sure that your company will pay for the classes <u>before</u> you register for classes or pay the tuition.

One of the things students should do is maximize the benefits once you are approved for the educational assistance. You can take courses that are eligible for college credit so that you can transfer the credits into a degree program.

Look for low-cost options, affordable one-time courses that will help you use the credit towards your degree program without having to take out any extra loans. You can also try to take some free trial courses to gauge yourself to see if you are ready for college. This way you minimize the risk of going through the process of getting the education assistance only to drop out of school or not even start schooling.

It is important to measure your progress. You can do this by evaluating your career and the direction it is moving towards. You may find yourself eligible for a promotion or in a better position to be selected for new projects where you may use your new skills.

Educational assistance will not be included with your wages, tips and other compensation shown on the W-2 form.

Please take advantage of the education assistance reimbursement program offered by your employer because you are fortunate to have such benefit. Take advantage of this benefit and invest in yourself, please never leave money on the table and remember the benefit of an education is yours forever. Once you have it, the sky is not the limit and you have limitless opportunities.

Furthermore, as an immigrant, many doors of opportunity will open for you. Such opportunities as a promotion, which sometimes may come with flexible working hours, or work remotely.

Being hired as a second language applicant increases your ability to compete in the job market with other American graduates.

5

Taking A Closer Look At Possible Challenges

"Abuse is not love. Abuse is about control." - Domestic Violence Survivor

Intimate Partner Violence

Once you accomplish your educational goal, immigrants, especially women, may unfortunately experience domestic abuse from their spouse. The spouse may feel intimated and sometimes may threaten them with all sort of things.

If the immigrant family does not have proper documentation, the spouse may threaten them through isolation. The woman may not be allowed to speak to her family or associate with friends from her home country. The spouse may use intimidation by threatening to destroy her school certificates and even her legal papers, which may render the woman powerless. Without legal papers, she does not have any documentation to prove she is legally in this country. Sometimes the spouse may even threaten to not file documentation for the woman.

There is also economic abuse a woman may experience from their spouses. They could call the woman's job and falsely accuse her of anything—for example, they have a criminal record or a misdemeanor, or they are not documented, or even using false documents.

The final example is threatening the woman to hurt their children or take them away from her if she tries to call the police.

All these abusive situations may happen because one of the spouse's feels intimated by the other person's education or achievement. This happens mainly to women immigrants, because of the stereotype mentality of most female immigrants should be taking care of the home—i.e. cooking, cleaning and making sure that the home runs smoothly.

While at school, I read this Journal of Women and Social Work from Sage Publishers, "Building Bridges to Safety and Justice: Stories of Survival and Resistance." In the journal, there was an immigrant lady from Africa going through abuse while still at school. She moved to another state, found a man who was from the same country, and thought that she was safe with him. They dated while she was going to graduate school, moved in together, got pregnant and had a baby.

The man became abusive and would not help her with the baby when she needed to go to school. One day the man just asked her flat out, "Why do you want to go to school anyway? Just sit at home with the baby, that's all I want from you." The spouse tried everything to stop her from going to school. He threatened to get her deported and finally they had to part ways. She went to the homeless shelter, where she got help and was moved to an apartment where she finally finished school and graduated.

The immigrant woman who is equipped with an education and a well-paying job, sometimes the job could be demanding and she may come home late or work on shifts—especially if she is in the health care field. This makes it hard for most women to do the things they were doing or done by women back in their home country. It gets a little bit challenging due to the work conflicts.

Unlike back in the home country, where we have house help and relatives who stay with you and help you with the housework. My advice to those who are going through any type of domestic abuse is please seek help. Here is the website and a toll-free number you can call: National Domestic Violence Hotline | 1-800-799-7233 | www.thehotline.org.

It is very interesting that the discussion about going or not going back to school is a family matter which is discussed and decided by both the husband and wife. Usually the family agrees on who may either go first or who the couple feels would make the greatest impact on the family. The family goes through some challenges (financial or emotional) during this period of schooling.

Financial Stress

"What really matters is not whether we have problems, but how we go through them. We must keep going on to make it through whatever we are facing" - Rosa Parks

Financial challenges could come in the form of the spouse going to school, taking less hours from work, and is now earning less and the family has to cut down on some things they used to have in the home. This financial challenge may also force the spouse who is not going to school to take more hours at work to cover the expenses, which otherwise could have been covered by the other spouse working.

Sometimes the family has to cut down on many things just to be able to live a comfortable life. Unless the student got financial help through the available channel mentioned above, financial challenges may also force the family to go into debt, using credit cards to make ends meet.

Sometimes when financial challenges creep in, marital stress starts, and if care is not taken, the marriage may fall apart. During that time the couple may be facing some economic challenges such as worries about employment, housing, bills, parenting and healthcare. Financial stress and strain may have an impact on both the husband and the wife, and may result in relationship pressure. It is very important to talk about financial matters in a supportive and constructive manner to enable the successful management of their financial matters. Both partners must understand the situation they are in and accept it, and agree that this is a temporary situation. Once school is done, they will bounce back to their normal financial life or even better.

Emotional Stress

"Change the way you look at things and the things you look at change." - Dr. Wayne Dyer

One of the major challenges the couple may face is emotional unavailability. The spouse who is going to school may be too busy with studies that managing time becomes a problem. At the same time, they could be having a lot of school work and the other person may not understand why they are not getting the attention they were not getting or the attention they are expecting.

As a student, sometimes when you are going through school as an adult, it gets tough because you have a lot going on—school, family, and work can be overwhelming. You can easily get emotionally stressed.

In as much as the individual going to school goes through emotional stress, the members of the family could also be going through emotional stress too. The children will be missing the attachment they had with that parent before the school journey started—the morning routines, the pillow fights, bedtime stories, and occasionally missing dinners and school activities.

The spouse could also be emotionally stressed. The spouse's attention has moved from them to books and they no longer have the relaxing time alone. For example, the candle-lit dinners diminish because half of the time the other spouse is engulfed with school work. If it's the wife, then she has to take care of the home, children and then books. By the end of the day, she is all drained out.

So, you see, though there are possible challenges with moving to the U.S. and pursuing a higher education, there are also opportunities to help you and your family through those challenges. And success is just a research and resource away!

6

Turning Lemons Into Lemonade

"Knowledge is power. Information is liberating. Education is the premise of progress, in every society, in every family." - Kofi Annan

As mentioned earlier in this book, immigrant women are those who were not born in the United States—this consists of legal permanent residence, naturalized citizens, refuges, asylum seekers and migrants who are in the United States temporarily.

Currently, we have more female than male immigrants in the United States, which makes about 21 million female immigrants, which is 13% of the total female population in the United States.

Statistics show that 19.7% of the immigrant woman are more likely to live in poverty than female citizens who were born in the U.S., and 66.3% are less likely to have health insurance coverage.

There is a need to change these statistics. We can do this through education, advocacy and empowering each other.

Immigrant women are able to self-define, develop transnational perspectives and have agency, that being the case we can do this together. For every 97 immigrant men there are 100 women, we have the numbers and we are a force to reckon with.

Therefore, we can change these statistics by encouraging women to go back to school and get that GED/certificate or diploma that will propel them to the next level. A better job results in better healthcare benefits!

Here are a few benefits of having a good U.S.-based education should you decide to move here. Keep in mind that this is not a comprehensive list of benefits, but these are a good start! Master these and you are well on your way to sustaining you and your entire family.

Education As An Investment

"Investment in knowledge pays the best interest." - Benjamin Franklin

Sometimes immigrants may not climb the corporate ladder because they have foreign credentials. It is hard for the employer to really understand what your qualifications equate to. Half of the time when you land in the U.S., regardless of your educational background or work experience, you may end up starting a job at the entry level, or may be required to do a certification before you can get placed.

Therefore, having an education from U.S. universities or colleges will give you a level playing ground with other qualified co-workers. You will also have the opportunity for promotion and the ability to apply for any job openings that come available at your job or outside your job. Therefore, you have a great chance of increasing your income.

With an education, you become more independent and knowledgable. It comes with some level of confidence which boosts your morale and performance. Because you have gone through school in the U.S., you are able to help your children navigate the system and help them make better choices in regards to subjects, school or even a career. You will understand the system better, and find it easy to navigate.

When we come to immigration issues, education is key not only here in the U.S., but also back in your country of origin. In the event that you find yourself back in your country of origin, you will be well equipped to find any type of employment as well us all the experience received while in the U.S.

It may not be easy but you are better off going back with a diploma from the U.S. than going back the way you came. The competition is tight, and it is not easy to just land back in your country of origin and get a job, but landing with a diploma from U.S. may open doors for you.

There are other professions that the employer may be able to file documentations for immigrants to become a U.S. citizen even though these are far and few, it's sort of like a work visa. But you can imagine if you have the qualifications the job requires and you happen to get the job, you saved yourself the stress of trying to be legal.

The immigrant faces a lot of challenges in American society today, be it discrimination or anti-immigration rhetoric. Therefore we must be cognizant of what we can do as immigrants to turn the lemons into lemonade. One of the things we must do is get an education if and when we can. Education is a lifelong investment. Nobody can take it away from you, neither can anybody deny that you have what it takes after going through school and achieving your academic goals.

Pillar For Growth

"Develop a passion for learning. If you do, you will never cease to grow." - Anthony J. D'Angelo

Once you get the education, you will be aiming higher and looking for those opportunities that will pay you well and better than what you were getting paid before. This means your income bracket may change. Once it changes and you start earning more, you will be able to start thinking about investments.

First, you may decide to buy a home or if you already have a house, you may decide to either upgrade the existing house or buy a new home in a better neighborhood. Good neighborhoods come with good school districts. Therefore, the kids get to go to better schools thereby getting a quality education. Sometimes, depending on your income, you may decide to put your children in private schools.

Additionally, most immigrants tend to invest back home, and you can only do this when and if you have an extra income. Because of the extra income, you may decide to have some income-building business back home, which will help the society by creating employment as well as building wealth for yourself. You will also able to help your relatives and parents. This becomes a win-win situation; you are comfortable here as well as your parents back home.

Good Life

"You get in life what you have the courage to ask for." - Oprah Winfrey

Financial stability brings financial well-being. Once you are financially stable, you are able to enjoy your life. You will be able to afford health insurance or get health care coverage through your employer. You will be able to plan for vacations and trips, able to feed your family well and dress well.

Depending on your financial need or circumstances, you may not need to do two to three jobs to make ends meet. You can get one well-paying job that can sustain you and you are able to live a fulfilling life. You will have more time with your spouse/partner, thus creating a fruitful relationship with your family.

The children will no longer be spending long hours alone without a parent or an adult at home to supervise or watch over them, especially after school and over the weekends. You will be there to help with their homework. Sometimes children face a lot of stress at school and when they get home, they would like to have somebody to talk to; and if you as a parent are not there, most of them do not know where to channel that stress. They may start having behavioral issues as a result of not having anyone there to listen to them. Studies have shown that some of the children who are left home alone develop delinquent behaviors and also start getting into bad company.

Having financial stability heals so many areas in our homes, and relieves a great deal of stress brought on by adjusting to this new land, going to U.S. school, and managing life and family in general. The good life is being able to make the financial stress lessen by getting a good education, thus affording the good job.

Molding the Children

"That idea that so many immigrants have to give their kids a better chance, they're the real success stories." - Narciso Rodriguez

Children learn through modeling and observation. They will always do what they have observed their parents do. Therefore, the more time you have with your children the better for them. Use the time to teach them some values, societal norms, virtuous beliefs and cultural traditions. Now that you have time on your hands, spend time instilling some values in your children.

Mothers, use the time to teach your children how to cook, this applies to both boys and girls. Teach them to cook traditional ethnic food. If you are not sure of how to do it, look among your network or support group. You could even sign-up for cooking classes for the family.

Parents, teach your children about cleanliness. There is a saying that 'cleanliness is close to godliness'. Work with them, showing them how it is done, and tell them why it's important to be clean and to be in a clean environment.

Fathers, use the time to have conversations with your sons about what society and family expects of a man. Talk to them about being responsible, accountable and dependable. Also teach them how they should treat their wife and/or children. This is very important because these values are being eroded.

Mothers, in the same way, use the time to talk to your daughters. Teach them how to take care of themselves and what society and family members expect of them. Have those mother-daughter conversations, let them feel comfortable talking to you about their fears and desires.

As parents, do things together at home like watching TV together, or having dinner together as a family is a good thing. You are showing the children the importance of the family unit. Sometimes as a family you may decide to take the children back home for summer vacation to stay with their grandparents, where they will learn more about their culture and traditions.

What your children learn about their culture and traditions come from you, as the parents. Teach them to be proud from where they come and all of the opportunities afforded to them as a result of hard work and dedication - from the family unit!

Conclusion

"For to be free is not merely to cast off one's chains, but to live in a way that respects and enhances the freedom of others."
– Nelson Mandela

As immigrants, it is very important that we go to school and better ourselves and take good care of our families. We must also not lose our culture, values, norms and beliefs. Therefore, it is critical to be vigilant on how we carry out our daily lives, and how we carry our parental duties as well.

With some extra education, you may have more time to spend with family, and this will help the unity of the family. Financial stress has an impact on marital and family relationships. Therefore, striving to make life better by doing a certification or getting a diploma will go a long way in saving the marriage and family from stress.

Emotional stress may go down since both parents may not be home to offer the children emotional support. As immigrants, we need to support one another as well as support the children. Immigrant children should not develop low self-esteem, low confidence levels and a negative view of themselves just because there was nobody at home to nurture them.

Give them affirmations and listen to what they are going through. We need to educate our young girls and boys on dangers of human trafficking, as we know human traffickers most often than not target immigrant women—therefore it's important to talk and encourage our young people not to be lured by cheap gains and to focus on their studies which adds a long term benefit to their life.

I just want to encourage all immigrants to research educational funding to enable you to get a certificate or a diploma that will make it easy for you to get to the next level.

If it does not work in the U.S., you can always use it when you go back to your country of origin. Also, look for organizations or companies that will pay for your education, that way you don't have to worry about loans to pay after completing your studies.

I am not suggesting that this is the only way you can make it in the U.S., but this is my opinion and my experience. Always have an exit strategy that benefits you and your family. As we know, the world has become a small village. With education, you will be able to get employment anywhere in the world. You can use your experience and skills anywhere in the world today.

Despite the susceptibilities, hurdles and sometimes abuse in the workplace that immigrants in general face, we still continue to make important contributions to our societies and economy—not only here but also in our country of origin. Therefore, we make a big impact in our communities.

"There must be a reason why I lived in all these lands, survived all those water crossing, while others fell from bullets or shut their eyes and simply willed their lives to end." - Chimamanda Ngozi Adichie

About the Author

Francisca Ramoni, Ph.D., is a Certified Family Life Educator and the founder of 'Empowering You', an organization that empowers communities one family at a time.

Empowering You is a uniquely dynamic group that promotes community development by providing motivation, education and social skills that advocates for financial literacy and financial well-being. Dr. Ramoni has over 15 years working in a financial institution and has been involved in many major projects.

Currently, Dr. Ramoni is Assistant Vice President with one of the major top banks in the USA, and is also currently an adjunct professor at Texas Woman's

University, a member of Women Graduate USA, and a member of National Society of Leadership & Success.

Dr. Ramoni is a recipient of the National Engaged Leader Award (NELA) 2018. Dr. Ramoni was nominated for the "Who's Who Among Students in American universities and colleges 2012".

Her accomplishments, skills, educational background, and training reflect a commitment to the advocacy for embracing diversity, valuable financial development, financial well-being and financial knowledge on the job. She believes that Financial Literacy is an essential component for increasing individual's financial well-being; empowering families is the gateway to having resilient and well-informed communities; and that education is power, education opens doors.

Dr. Ramoni earned both her Doctor of Philosophy in Family Studies and Master's degree in Child Development from Texas Woman's University; and a Master's degree in Financial management and Institutions, Bachelor's degree in Commerce - Statistics both from India.   Dr. Ramoni's dissertation was on financial literacy among young adults.

Some of Dr. Ramoni's publications underway are:

Financial Literacy: Parental influence on financial literacy among young adults.

Financial Literacy: The importance of parental influence on financial literacy among young adults.

Financial Literacy: Are young adults well equipped to face the current economic world?

The Legacy *of an*

IMMIGRANT WOMAN

Unmasking the opportunities available but hidden in plain sight that will lead to success in a new and strange land

-THE END-

www.ingramcontent.com/pod-product-compliance
Lightning Source LLC
Chambersburg PA
CBHW070759250726
48662CB00004B/1893